Mother Angelica Talks It Over

Also by Mother Angelica

*Praying with Mother Angelica: Meditations on the Rosary,
the Way of the Cross, and Other Prayers*

Mother Angelica's Answers, Not Promises

Mother Angelica on Christ and Our Lady

Mother Angelica on Suffering and Burnout

Mother Angelica on God, His Home, and His Angels

Mother Angelica's The Way of the Cross

Mother Angelica's Quick Guide to the Sacraments

Mother Angelica's Guide to Practical Holiness

A Holy Hour with Mother Angelica

Mother Angelica on Prayer and Living for the Kingdom

Mother Angelica's Guide to the Spiritual Life

Mother Angelica's Lessons on Genesis

What Is Heaven?

In His Sandals: A Journey with Jesus

Living the Scriptures

Mother Angelica's Keys to the Interior Life

Mother M. Angelica

Mother Angelica
Talks It Over

Edited by Daniel Hopkins

EWTN Publishing, Inc.
Irondale, Alabama

EWTN Publishing, Inc.
5817 Old Leeds Road, Irondale, AL 35210

Distributed by Sophia Institute Press, Box
5284, Manchester, NH 03108.

paperback ISBN 978-1-68278-409-9
ebook ISBN 978-1-68278-410-5

Library of Congress Control Number: 2025933387

First printing

Contents

Family Problems

We're going to talk about the triple agony of having problems in your family life.

For example, when something is wrong in the family, parents suffer a lot. The individual that's kind of goofing off suffers a lot. Children suffer a lot. Each part of that family has a different kind of pain, and it is in understanding their pain of each other that sometimes we can be brought together.

And I want to take a little bit of Scripture here from St. Luke's Gospel. Our Lord said that there was a woman who had ten drachmas and she lost one. She lit a lamp, searched the house thoroughly until she found it. And when she found it, she called her neighbors together and said, "Rejoice with me. I have found the drachma I have lost" (15:9). And He gave this as an example of the Kingdom. And you see, a parent that has his son or a daughter that has just strayed from the right path—it's like that woman that had ten drachmas. She may have other children. She may have other concerns. But she sweeps. She hunts. She does everything possible. She finds that one.

We learn from St. Augustine's life and his mother, St. Monica, who prayed for her son for thirty years. That's a lot of time, isn't it? I don't know if I'd persevere that long. With my Italian temperament, I think after two or three years, I'd say, "Oh, get lost. You want to go, go." Maybe I would do that. Maybe I wouldn't. I hope I wouldn't. But she didn't. She just kept on and on. And she just bugged the Lord until her son began very slowly—and that's another aspect of our life together, we must give people time to grow.

You know, there's a little plaque that says: "Be patient with me. God's not through with me yet." See, God isn't through with any of us yet. So we want to look at the agonies of parents when their sons or their daughters are in addiction, alcohol, ran away from home—whatever the problem is, we want to look at them. We want to look at the child. And today, we want to look at the other member of the family who sometimes thinks, "Gee, look, I'm here too."

You know, how come all our attention is geared toward So-and-so, who's goofing off all the time? So they have a very special kind of agony. And until we realize each other's problems, we're just never going to be loving because we won't see God in any of it. See, we won't understand why God permits this stuff in our life. It's like being put in a fire. We don't want to be put in a fire. But you know, if we just had a clump of coal, that wouldn't manner, it wouldn't mean anything. But you want to make it into a necklace. You want it to look beautiful. You got to put some fire to that thing, it's got to be molded. And when you mold, what do you do? When you mold, you squeeze. It takes pain. It takes suffering. It takes a lot of patience. Patience. And that's something we don't have. We belong to an instant generation—an instant generation that says, "Well, if I can't have it now, I don't want it."

See, the best things in life are not instant. God works sometimes in your soul. He makes you think He isn't around. Sometimes I look at God and say, "Hey, what is it? You went on a vacation or what? You don't hear me down here? You're everywhere, and You don't hear me?" See now, we all have our problems. But if we share these problems together in the Lord, then we're going to come out just right.

Sometimes you look at God, and there's only the two of us. "There's just no one else, Lord." And sometimes He has to almost get you down to that level so you can look up and say, "Lord, help me."

We're just stubborn people sometimes. And sometimes without our fault, you just have to reach out and say, "Lord, I don't understand. I don't know what's going on, but I know You love me. And I believe in that love, and I believe in Your caring."

God bless you all.

Helping to Bring People
Back to the Church

We're going to ask a very, very important question. That is, why do you stay away? There are people who have stayed away from the Church for years and years and years. We've got to find out why. We have to ask them why.

There's a little passage here in the Acts of the Apostles. It says, if you remember, there was a eunuch that was studying the Scriptures, but he didn't know what he was studying, and nobody talked to him about it. And so the Lord took Philip, just placed him next to this carriage, and Philip ran up to the eunuch, who was reading the prophet Isaiah, and he said, "Do you understand what you're reading?" And he said, "How can I unless someone guides me? Unless someone tells me?" (see Acts 8:30–31).

You know, I don't think we understand that, as Christians and Catholics, we're obliged to preach the Word, to be an example, and to talk to people about coming home. You know, if someone has left the Church, you kind of say, "Hmm, I wonder what you did?" But we never say, "Why did you leave?" See, perhaps our neighbor who has left his church is so hurt. There are many, many reasons. And we're going to discuss the reasons why people stay away from the Church. But our obligation as a Christian, as a Catholic, is to be so concerned that we will run with him and say, "Hey! Why don't you come home?"

But you see, the word *home* is not always given to the Church. And the Church is a home. The Church is a Mother. We say Holy Mother Church. Always run to your Mother. We had some teenagers here, and we asked them, "If you were in trouble, where would you go?"

They said, "I'd go to a friend."

I said, "Well, your friend doesn't know any more than you do."

"I know that."

"So, why wouldn't you go to the Church?"

I found it very, very strange that they said they would not go to the Church. And I realized something. We have not portrayed the Church as Mother. We have not said, "Look, she is a Mother, and she cares for you."

And you see, since you are the Church, do you show that care for your neighbor? Do you show that care? You know, we're in evangelization, with our books — we've been for years — and we have had people go door-to-door in some of our big cities. And a person would open the door and take this little leaflet that talked about God, just talked about the Lord, His attributes, whatever we were talking about. And they would say, "Nobody ever gave me one before. Nobody cared." And you and I, as Catholics and Christians, have to begin to be evangelistic, not by telling people what to do but by caring. To say, "You don't go to church? Why?" Don't be afraid of their answer. They may have all kinds of reasons. We have chocolate-coated reasons, and we have bitter reasons; we have bittersweet reasons. We have all kinds. Some are just too lazy. We just don't want to get up early in the morning. But you can go to Mass almost any time. Go to Mass Saturday, Sunday night. But even then, we have excuses.

But then we don't portray that there is something you're missing. And that's another thing. We don't have enthusiasm. Oh, there are some people I would like to put a match under. Just so you move. When you're enthused about something, when you're enthused about your mother, you're going to talk about your mother. You're going to talk a lot about your mother. You're going to say, "Hey, I got the best mom in the world. Why don't you come see her?" If you're in trouble, when your neighbor is in trouble, do you say, "Go to church"? "Oh, that's an institution; that's a structure." No! You run to your mother when you're in trouble. And you see, our neighbor, chances are, has so many heartaches that he can't even begin to tell you about them, and you don't have time to listen.

But if he knows you care and he knows he has a mother to go to, you're okay.

There are many people who don't go to church because they feel they just are not perfect enough. Maybe we've portrayed our saints as so perfect, so without fault, that you just can't come up to them.

And then there are those who, well, they just don't want to go or they feel that there has been a bad example. That bad example is so prevalent among laypeople.

So, whatever reason you don't go to church, come on home. We love you just as you are.

God bless you.

Faith

We're going to talk about faith. I think it's a very, very misunderstood virtue.

We're going to look at St. Paul in Hebrews. He says in the eleventh chapter, "Only faith can guarantee the blessings that we hope for, or prove the existence of the realities that at the present time remain unseen" (v. 1).

And you see, today, we are a generation of seeing people. If you can't see it, if you don't understand it, it doesn't exist. So that means you limit yourself to your own intelligence. I don't know how you can even begin to accept God as God if you're going to limit Him to what you understand.

Now, our concept of faith today sometimes means that I accept the teachings of the Church. And that's true. I accept the Trinity. I accept the Immaculate Conception. I accept all these beautiful truths of the Church. But then there is that everyday, nitty-gritty faith. That's what trips you up. Does God want me to do this? Do I have faith to see in this terrible situation that to me is a tragedy—a heartache—at least that there is God? "You mean that God is in this miserable situation?" Now, that kind of faith we have a hard time with.

Do you have a hard time with that? I do. I don't have any problem with the Trinity. I have a problem seeing God sometimes in mean people, in situations that are so unfair. I have a hard time seeing with the eyes of faith when I see that things aren't moving. See, being Italian by descent is a terrible handicap because you've got to have everything done yesterday. It takes a lot of faith to see that God is going to make you wait.

So you put reasons on people. You say, "Well, if this man or this woman or this organization will just get with it, get off their chairs and do something!" You see, here we put all these reasons on everything. And so practical faith, the kind of faith that says, "I see

Jesus," and then the faith that sees Jesus in my neighbor—I don't mind seeing Jesus in a nice neighbor. In nice neighbors, you can see Jesus. They're kind, they're loving, they're sweet, they're understanding. But the neighbor that isn't any of these things—to be able to see and to love Jesus like Mother Teresa does in the very low, "the least," the Lord says, takes a lot of faith. And faith is to see the invisible reality.

And that's why some people today only live half a life. The human life. The life they can see. A thing they can understand. But they never get to the invisible reality that in this place there is the Lord God—Father, Son, and Holy Spirit—that in this temple (us), be it ever so imperfect, be it ever so faulty, is God. To see that all these people embody the Trinity—that takes a lot of faith. I've got to go beyond your eyes and your face and your hair and your intelligence. And I've got to see that invisible but ever present and real reality. And that's what we have a hard time with today.

And you have a hard time with that. I know you do.

There is in the Church a tremendous amount of faith, a tremendous amount of devotion. And we want you to know that if you believe in Jesus, you have the greatest gift God could have ever given you because you have with you always a presence unseen, but very real and very loving.

God bless you.

Chosen by God

We're going to talk about being chosen. We all know that we've been chosen. We're not always aware of that choice.

And I want to look at Isaiah 43 in the Scriptures. He says, "Do not be afraid, for I have redeemed you. I have called you by your name. You are mine" (v. 1).

Just imagine that. God calling you by your own name.

You know, the most flattering thing is if someone very famous comes up to you, that you maybe met once, and he says, "Hello, Mrs. Smith, how are you?" And you think, "Oh, he knew me! He remembered." But just imagine God.

I'm going to share a little experience with you about perhaps two or three years ago after Communion. I was just making my thanksgiving, and suddenly it was if my soul just kind of popped out of my body, and it found itself on a sphere, like a world—huge. And I was all alone with this very, very strange experience. And I seemed to be all alone on this sphere. And I was aware of nothingness. And all my life I used to wonder, "What is nothingness?" I've never known nothingness because everything I have, everything I've seen, is something.

So, it was very difficult for me to understand nothingness. Suddenly, I found myself on this sphere, and I was aware of nothingness. And I was aware that there was just a being—it was something. Yet I was aware of nothing. And it was as if my soul was crying out. And I could remember that it used to echo; it'd say, "Yahweh!" And there was no response.

And this went on for days. And it was a really strange experience because I was able to function; like I could talk to people and do my work and do everything, except in my soul there was always this experience. It was like being and not being at the same time. Really, really strange experience.

And I began to write it down. It's in a book called *Before Time Began*. But as it progressed, as this experience went on, one day I realized that there were other nonbeings with me, and I was aware there were millions and millions and millions of other people like me waiting in this nothingness. And it was a kind of wonder.

And then this went on for days. And then suddenly I was aware for the first time of a presence—a very loving presence. And I realized that it was God. And all through this experience, every so often I could hear my soul cry out to God, wanting some kind of attention. "Is there someone there?" And there were all these other beings out there, and my soul used to cry out, "Yahweh!" And you could hear this echo into nothingness. And then I suddenly realized that this warm, loving, gentle presence began to hover, began to move over these millions and millions and millions of other human beings. And as it moved, they no longer were. And it moved, and they just ceased to be.

And it was a strange, strange experience because I could feel the presence coming towards me. And I wondered in my soul whether or not I would cease to be. Doesn't this sound crazy? That you knew you were and yet you had that definite feeling that there was that chance that you wouldn't be.

And so finally, I could feel that presence coming over me. And it stopped. And it was like holding the breath you didn't have. And suddenly It said, "You shall be." And I realized that God gave me the experience of having been in His thought, and He made the decision. He made that decision that out of a possible billion, billion, billion, billion, billion human beings that might have been, God chose me to be. Isn't that terrific?

It was a kind of terrifying experience. But when I read this passage, every time I read it, that whole experience seems to come back to me. And that's why the sisters, as I was going through it, made me put it into a little booklet form. But that really made me realize what Jeremiah was saying: "Before you were created in your mother's womb, I knew you" (1:5). But the most marvelous thing about that particular experience was that I had the definite feeling that there was that chance, there was definitely that chance, that I might not be chosen to be. And it was terrifying, and yet in the same way, when He said, "You shall be," I realized that very special choice that I *was*, and that you *were*.

And so no matter how miserable life might be and how unfair or unjust or whatever it is, you must realize that God has a very special love. He calls you by name, and He chose you to be, out of a possible sixty, seventy, eighty, ninety billion people who might have been.

God is working today in such wonderful ways, that you and I just have to be awestruck because the Spirit is not outdone in generosity.

Spirituality for the Young

We're going to talk about spirituality for teenagers and children. And this doesn't seem to be appropriate, but I think it is because we've got to start very, very small.

It says here in 2 Timothy, "I have fought the good fight. I have run the race to the finish. I have kept the faith" (see 4:7).

We've got to begin very young talking to God and talking with God. Because if we don't, if we let God out of anything in our life, then, you see, you're kind of a little bit on your own, and you're not as in union with God if you don't let Him in on the every everyday thing.

I'm going to give an example. A woman came one day for counseling a few years ago, and she had a little leaguer there, you know, just a tiny little fella. He had a little suit on, and I knew he was going to go somewhere. He was very nervous. And she was talking about her problems, and he kept pulling at her, and he wanted to talk to me, and she kept pushing him aside.

And finally, when she was through, he said, "I want to talk to Mother."

And I thought, "Hey, he's got a problem, and he's just *that* tall."

And so I said, "What can I do for you, honey?"

And he said, "I want to hit a home run."

I said, "You want to *what?*"

"I want to hit a home run."

And I said, "You play baseball?"

He said, "Yes." And he told me he lost every game of the season. He never won a game that whole season. And he wanted to hit a home run. And he wanted to know if I prayed for home runs.

And I said, "Oh, sure, I pray for everything."

And his mother looked at me, like, "You're kidding."

So, I said, "Jim, honey, you want to hit a home run?"

He said, "Yes."

And I said, "Okay, tell you what you do. The next time you go up to bat, you take that bat in your hand and you say, 'Jesus, hit that ball.'"

And he looked at me, and his eyes got big, and he said, "Will it work?"

And I said, "Sure."

And he said, "Okay."

Well, a week later, I forgot all about it. Then I got a phone call, and Sr. Michael came in and she said, "There must be a tiny fella on the phone because his voice is very high-pitched and sounds very young, and he wants to talk to you."

I didn't know who it was.

So, I went there. I said, "Hello?"

He said, "Mother Angelica?"

I said, "Yes."

He said, "I hit a home run!"

And I said, "What did you do?"

He said, "I saw that ball coming, and I said, 'Jesus, hit that ball.'" And he said, "You should have seen it go!"

And I thought, "Oh, thank You, Lord."

That's three cheers for the Lord, isn't it? So what I'm trying to say is don't let Jesus out of your home runs. Don't let Him out of anything. Don't let Him out of your failures. Don't let Him out of anything in your life, whether you're looking for a parking place or whether you're going to hit a home run or whether you have an exam.

Students are great for prayer before exams. They goof off all week, all semester, and they get very holy right before exams. So you don't want to do that. Oh, you do, but you want to bring Jesus in on everything. If there's something in your life you don't want Him to know about or see, then that tells you something, doesn't it? When you can't talk to your friend about the problem because you're that ashamed or afraid? So let Him in on every aspect of your life.

Whether it's peer pressure in school, with dope addiction, or peer pressure in your office with fellow executives, or peer pressure being a plumber—whatever the pressure is—you need to know that with Jesus you can stand alone. Because with Him as your Friend, you possess the whole wide world.

God bless you.

Living with Jesus

We're going to talk about my favorite subject and your favorite subject: Jesus.

You know, a lot of people today don't understand what Christianity is all about. They think it's a big club, and you go to church on Sunday to render homage to God—just in case. Besides, that's the thing to do.

But between Sunday and Sunday, we put Him in a little box, and we pull Him out every time we need something. We say, "Yoo hoo, I need You." And then we zip Him back, and that's the end of it until we need something else. But that isn't why Jesus came. I want to read you something. I get excited every time I hear it.

Scripture says, "I will ask the Father, and He will give you a Paraclete to be with you forever—the Spirit of Truth. Now, the world cannot receive Him, and it neither sees Him nor knows Him, but you know Him." And you know why you know Him? "Because He is with you and *in* you" (see John 14:16–17).

You know what we call that? We call that the *divine indwelling*. Now, this is not imaginary. Through the power of the Spirit, the power of grace, the whole Trinity lives in you. Can you imagine that? You know why we have a hard time with that? Because we're so faulty.

I had a little talk with some fifth graders one time, and I said, "How many want to go to Heaven?" Everybody lifted up their hand except one little fella. And I looked at him, and I said, "Don't you want to go to Heaven?" And he said, "None of this gang is going."

We just don't have a concept of Heaven within us. Why? Because St. Paul says we're earthenware vessels. We get all tangled up in the flak, in the imperfections, in the weaknesses. And we lose sight of the beauty and the dignity of our souls. You and I are a temple of the Lord. You carry Jesus around you and within you. And that's why it's so necessary for you to radiate. You've got to radiate. That's why a sad saint is no saint at all.

And one of our problems with sanctity is that you think sanctity is to be perfect, right? I know you do. And that's why, when your neighbor is the least bit imperfect, you say, "He could never be holy." Or you look at someone and say, "I thought you were a Christian." What does that mean: "I thought you were a Christian"? Because you lost your temper, you're a little bit hard to get along with.

In the great times of the Church in which St. Mechtilde and St. Gertrude were living, St. Mechtilde had a vision of the Lord, and she said, "Lord, which one of the nuns in this monastery is most pleasing to You?" Because she thought He was going to say, "You." And He didn't. He said, "If you want to find me, look in the heart of Gertrude." And she was horrified. And she said, "Gertrude! That impatient individual?" And the Lord said, "Look." And He showed her Gertrude. And Gertrude was like a person with a revolving head. And no matter where she went, no matter what she did, she was conscious of the awesome presence of God in her neighbor and herself.

And though she struggled and struggled to get rid of impatience—that's why she's my favorite saint, see; I like saints that are impatient and struggle and have hot tempers. I want somebody like me. I want somebody that has to struggle from the time they put their feet out of bed in the morning to the time they get in bed at night.

I want somebody who has to struggle to be with Jesus and to live with Jesus because I think that's where it's at. I think you and I are in a constant struggle; however, we've got all that power in here, all that power to live with Jesus. That is the most growing experience. And it's not always easy because it's a decision.

You didn't think it was a decision, huh? You thought it was a big, fat feeling, didn't you? No, it's a decision. It's on the will level. I must *will* to be with Jesus. That doesn't mean I desire it. You can desire a lot of things, but you never get them done. It means I make every effort to realize the beauty in your soul.

So it doesn't matter what your color is, what your knowledge is. If you're a human being, I see Jesus in you. And I like this. I like to have the Father in me and see Jesus in you. You know what happens? When that happens, the Spirit comes. So when I see Jesus in you and you see Him in me, then love begins to blossom. No matter how difficult it is.

When you love Jesus, you're going to do, you're going to be with, and you're going to have confidence in His will.

Fear and Faith

We're going to talk about fear and faith and just a lot of things.

I'm going to read to you something from St. Mark's Gospel (4:35-40). Our dear Lord had one of those days, and He decided to go and get away from it all. And so He said, "Let's cross over to the other side." And so, they got into the boat.

And it says here it began to blow a gale. And the waves were breaking into the boat so that it almost was swamped.

Can you imagine that, huh? Here is this boat, and here is Jesus, and here are these apostles. They had just finished talking to a fantastic amount of people. Maybe four or five, six thousand people.

And they're elated. You know, when you talk about Jesus to a great big group of people, and they're all enthused, you go out, and I don't know about anybody else, but you get real enthused, and you're all excited. I go out and eat pizza after that. But Jesus got into a boat; see, He didn't have pizza to go for.

And so He went and got into a boat. So here are these apostles, and they're all excited. Suddenly, reality comes into being. And here comes a storm. But they're not too excited. After all, Jesus is there. Here comes a wave. And Peter looks at John. John looks at Peter. And he says, "There's a storm." And John says, "I know it."

And then here comes another wave. And the boat begins to fill with water. And Peter says, "The boat's filling with water." And John says, "Get a bucket." This is my rendition of Scripture; don't look for it in the book.

So here they are. And the boat's filling with water. And Peter says to John, "Wake the Master." Here Mark says that Jesus was at the stern of the boat, His head on a cushion, asleep. He was so tired.

I love to see, to realize, that God was tired. And you can't imagine anybody loving you so much that He'd want to feel tired. But there He was. He wanted to feel like you feel; He was just bushed; He was sound asleep.

And here's Peter. He doesn't understand God sleeping when he's almost drowning. So he says to John, "Wake the Master."

John says, "No."

"What do you mean no?"

He says, "No, He's tired."

And Peter says, "We're drowning!"

And John says, "I'm not going to wake Him up."

Here comes a big wave. And Peter says, "I said, 'Wake the Master!'"

And John said, "I said no."

Well, Peter, here comes another wave. And he is drenched, and the boat is almost to the sinking point, you know; it gets kind of light suddenly, and it begins to kind of bob up and down. And Peter does this. Peter goes, and he shakes Jesus. And he says, "Master, don't You care? We're drowning!"

Oh, wow! Can you imagine? There must have been silence in that boat. And you know what Jesus did? I bet you a nickel. He woke up very slow. I bet He woke up one eye at a time. And He looked at Peter finally. And He looked at the storm. And it must have seemed an infinite amount of time when He said, "Quiet. Be calm."

Then He looked at Peter. You know what He said to Peter? He says, "How is it you have no faith?" Now, He didn't say, "How is it you have a little faith?" Not, "How come you're a little shaky?" No. "How come you have no faith?"

Well, you and I sometimes ask God the same question. Have you ever said to Him, "Hey, don't You care?" I've said that to Him. I've said to Him, "Hey, wake up. I'm going down. The net is going down. We're starting to sink. Where are You?" And then He does something so nice. And I feel like a heel. I feel like two cents. And I go to the Blessed Sacrament, and I can hardly look at Him.

And He says to me, "Angelica, how come? How come you have no faith?" So, you and I have to look at faith. We have to look at what we call catechesis. We have to look at the structure and the nitty-gritty aspect of faith, what we call the Faith. We have to look at it and see how we really fare in the line of faith and hope and love.

God bless you.

Responding to God's Call

We're going to talk about responding to God's call, no matter what that call is, no matter what that vocation is.

We are going to look at St. Matthew's Gospel, and we find the parable of the talents (25:14–30). And the Lord said, "It is like a man on his way abroad who summoned his servants and entrusted his property to them. To one he gave five talents, to another two, to a third one" (25:14–15).

We all know the story. You know, the one that had five went out and made five more. The one who had two went out, and he made two more.

The one that had one—he thought, "Ah, the master is kind of hard. I might lose this thing. I might make something, but I might not. And then when he comes back, he's going to kill me if I don't make something out of this. I'm going to bury it. At least when he comes back up, I'll give it back to him. No problems. Didn't lose anything, didn't make anything, but he didn't lose anything."

And we all know what happened. The master came back, and he said, "Okay, I gave you a talent, what do you got?"

He said, "Look, I know you. You're a man who reaps what he doesn't sow. So, I buried it. Here it is. Take it. God bless you. Thanks for letting me have it. Take it back."

The master was angry. He said, "Ah, you wicked servant! Why didn't you at least put it in the bank for interest?" They had interest even then—can you beat that? Times haven't changed at all.

You and I, my friends, whatever vocation you are, whether you're a married vocation, career, single, religious, a priest, minister, whatever—we have to understand that God gives us talents, and we've got to use those talents. We're going to be accountable.

You can't bury them and say, "Oh, now, this is too risky."

See, today we have no longer a theology of risk. We want everything nice and comfortable and assured. *Got* to have assurance. You got to be sure it's going to succeed. You don't want anybody to think you tried something and failed. You never want to fail. But you see, the whole gospel is one risk after another. So if the Lord gives you a vocation to be a Christian, that's a risk—because you stand up sometimes, you stand up tall, and you stand up alone. *Alone.* In your office, for example, people go around telling dirty jokes, and you decide not to. You stand alone. You're living up to your vocation. You are saying to God, "You have given me the talent of Christianity, and I'm going to live up to that talent."

And some of us, you know, we're just not going to do that. We're aiming for Purgatory. Most Catholics aim for Purgatory, and you hear people say, "Well, if I just get in the gate, if I just get in the gate." If you're aiming for the gate, buddy, I have news for you: you may not make it. And then what are you going to do?

Don't be afraid to surrender. Surrender to God. Don't be afraid to do that. Don't be afraid to say, "Look, I'm going to give You all. I'm going to take every risk that You want me to take." Be sure it's God who wants you to take it, though, or you're in real trouble.

Use your talents. Use all of your talents. Now, you know talents differ one from another, and sometimes we have talents we don't even know exist. Did you know it's a talent to smile? Did you ever think that was a talent?

Some people have an infectious smile. One time, I was going downtown; I had all kinds of worries on my mind, it looked like the whole world was falling in on me, as it does sometimes, and I was walking down the street. Sister and I were shopping, and I walked down, and here came a woman with just a tiny little child, must have been maybe three or four years old. And that child looked at me and smiled. That's all she did. And she gave me a smile from ear to ear, and it showed me Jesus. And I thought, "If that child smiles at anybody else today, if she goes on her whole life and does nothing else but smile, sometimes that's all you need."

Some of you that are in apartment houses and are widows, it seems sometimes that your whole life is just gone. You still have the talent of encouragement, the talent of giving people the benefit of your wisdom, your experience. That's very important. You can't substitute experience. You can talk a lot about a recipe, but there's nobody like a great cook. And so, you've got to put your experience to use in some area in convalescent homes and all the other places where you feel sometimes so helpless and useless. You're not. You have a great talent, the talent to give hope, the talent to witness to the Kingdom, the talent to smile, the talent to say to everyone, "I love you." And that is a great talent today because we're so afraid to love. We're so afraid to respond to God. We're so afraid to respond to our neighbor because we know there are going to be obligations with that.

God bless you. And remember, God is doing exciting things today and in you.

Playing God

We're gonna talk about playing God.

You think you play God once in a while? Do you make decisions for other people and try to figure out what God wants you to do at this moment, and you're absolutely sure that's what He wants you to do? And sometimes, of course, we are.

But St. Paul says here in 1 Corinthians, "We teach what scripture calls: the things that no eye has seen or no ear has heard... things that God has revealed to us through the Spirit, for the Spirit reaches the depths of everything, even the depths of God. The depths of a man can only be known by his own spirit, not by any other man" (2:9–11). We don't always remember that. And that's why we rash-judge people so much. Isn't that true? We rash-judge our neighbor. We're absolutely sure that he meant this or he meant that. I bet you all have somebody in mind that you really rash-judge, and you determine what his heart is, determine what his mind is, determine what he's going to do, determine what he should do or you think he should do. And I think what we do—I find myself doing this—you have a tendency to put everyone in your mold. You have no other mold, do you? No, you have no other mold but your own to judge by. So, if you're effervescent, you just don't know anybody would be calm about anything. And if you're very calm, you're very upset for somebody else who is effervescent. So, we try to push everybody in that mold. And of course, parents do that. And then we make decisions.

But this is why we do sometimes make decisions about people's lives, about their hearts, about their minds, their work. "My father's a doctor, so I have to be a doctor." Well, maybe you'd make a better plumber than a surgeon. We are so tied up; it's just phenomenal to see how tied up we are with our own ideas, and we don't have the faith anymore to let God evolve and to let our neighbor be as he is—his faulty self. And one day, we'll find out that we have a few peccadilloes of our own. That comes as a surprise, doesn't it, that you have a few faults?

You always think, "If my neighbor improved, I'd be so happy." See? "If my family were better." "My husband, my wife," whatever. In religious life, we have the same problem. There are days I want to throw all my sisters, all the crew, all the people I know right out the window because I think they're out to get me. And I'm sure of that. And when I get sure of that, then they just bug me to death. So they must improve. And I think that's why some of our religious have left their orders. They want the order to be exactly the way they want it to be or the way it was. We cannot adapt ourselves to changes in the Church, or we wanted to have Latin, and we wanted to do this, we wanted to do that, and now that we don't do it, I don't go anymore.

We've got to have everything the way we want it. So we play God. And this is something we need to look at sometimes and say, "Am I playing God? Or am I looking and trying to find God in my neighbor in all the situations of my life?"

I like to be like a little kid. The Lord said we should be as children. I'd like to be like a child and just marvel as God evolves events and people and how He takes up a lot of garbage sometimes and puts you in the middle of it, then suddenly makes it beautiful. We need to look at God and say, "Lord, I want You to run my life. I want You to be the center of my life. I want You to be uppermost in all I do, all I say, all I think." So that when people look at us as Christians, they *should* see the Jesus that we adore. They should see the Lord God in our actions. Because you are His hands and you are His feet. See, you want to be used by God in order to make the world a better place to live in.

God bless you. And remember, God is doing exciting things today and in you.

Evangelization

We're going to talk about evangelization.

Ordinarily, we think that ministers and priests and religious are the ones who are obliged to be evangelists, and the rest of us just go our way. But, you see, the example of the Christian is the biggest source of evangelization. In the Acts, it says that the pagans were converted not so much by the Word that was preached, but they looked and they said, "See how these Christians love one another." So, it was a matter of seeing something that you felt you lacked.

And today, you see Christians so unhappy. You see Christians so distressed. You see Christians almost in an attitude as if they had very little or no faith. And so, someone who is in the same situation perhaps looks at us and says, "Well, I don't see any difference. I see you just as unhappy and just as frustrated, just as worried about dying and everything else as I am. So what do you have?" The power of example.

Now, Jesus says here, in St. Matthew's Gospel, to the apostles: "Go and make disciples of all nations" (see 28:19). Now, we know that this is something that was given to these men as priests, that they were to go and baptize. But you and I, as Christians, are that beacon on top of a mountain. You and I are a light. You're a lighthouse. Now, a minister can preach all he wants to. But if his parishioners are not the epitome of what he preaches, then when someone comes into the Church, what does he find? That is the important thing. Once we convert someone, once we make someone know that there is a Jesus and that Jesus loves them, does he come into a church that is warm? Does he come into our family? Does he come into our fold? Does he feel in his heart that he belongs?

See, if we don't do that, if we don't have the warmth and the compassion of Jesus in our hearts—that is your obligation as a Christian. It doesn't matter who you are. It doesn't matter how old you are. It doesn't matter how young you are. It only matters that you preach by example. An example goes very far.

You know, in my monastery, a sister will come up to me and ask for some permission to do something that no one else is doing at the present moment. In about three days' time, I'll find five sisters doing exactly the same thing. And they don't have permission. None of them had permission to do it. I gave permission to one. But now I got five people doing exactly the same thing. You know, that is the power of example. And we don't realize how powerful it is.

And you got to evangelize your family before you evangelize anyone else. Did you know that? Your family needs evangelization. They need to see the presence of Jesus. That's what it means to evangelize. It doesn't mean only to say what is true. It doesn't only mean to say that there is a Lord. It means that you believe it to a point where your enthusiasm is catching.

See, we don't like enthusiasm. Sometimes I would like to put matches under Christians and just say,

"Move! Do something!" See, I want you to be enthused over your Christianity. That's what the apostles had. Can you imagine Paul being so, "Oh, well, there is a Lord, and I wish you'd know Him, everybody." Well, you wouldn't be attracted to that. He was a fiery man. All the apostles were fiery people. And you cannot love someone and not be fiery over that knowledge and wanting to share.

Today we're kind of selfish. We know Jesus, and we love Jesus. We go to church every Sunday, and then we want to hide it, and we're just all by ourself. They don't want you to share that. But you have to share. Love that is not shared is not love. Enthusiasm that is not open is not enthusiasm. So, you and I must look at ourselves and see: Are we evangelists? Are we preaching the Word?

We want you out there to know that our dear Lord loves you very much, and be enthusiastic about your Faith because Jesus is Lord and He loves you, and you just can't keep that a secret.

Rash Judgment

We're going to talk about judgment and how we rash-judge.

Now, you say, "Well, I never rash-judge." Oh, yeah, you do. And we're going to see what Our Lord has to say about it first.

He says in St. Luke's Gospel, "Be compassionate as the same way as your Father is compassionate. Do not judge, and you will not be judged yourselves. Do not condemn, and you will not be condemned either" (see 6:36–37).

Isn't that marvelous? Just think, if you never condemned in your whole life, the Lord wouldn't condemn you either. Can you beat that? When you meet Him for the first time after death, you could say, "I didn't condemn anybody." And He'd say, "Okay, y'all come." That's what He'd say.

Anyway, He says, "Grant pardon, and you will be pardoned. Give, and there will be gifts for you." Full measure, running over (see 6:37–38).

Now, there are some parts of Scripture that seem to contradict each other. It seems like Our Lord said one thing one time, something else another time. Another place, He says, "By their fruit, you know them" (see Matt. 7:20). Right? That's to judge. And here He says, "Do not judge, and you will not be judged."

So you say, "Well, Lord, now do you or don't you? See, I'm getting mixed up!" And no, He said both, and He meant both. Because what we judge is motives. You judge the heart. That's what you can never judge.

Now, if somebody hits another boy, you can't say, "I didn't see him do it." That would be a lie. So, the fruit says that's bad. You shouldn't sock your brother. Pull his hair a little bit, but don't sock him. Now, that is not judging. You see, you have seen something, it actually happens, when you're judging fruit, and you say, "Well, that's not good fruit; you shouldn't do that.

You should be compassionate, forgiving." But now you can't judge why he did it. And that's what we judge.

Do you ever hear somebody say, "I just know why she did it"? You say, "Why?" They put the most imaginary, the most colorful motives on your actions that you wouldn't even imagine you did it for that purpose.

I know two women who didn't talk to each other for two years. You know why? Because one was going down the street. She had a tooth pulled, and her jaw was all swollen, and her friend passed her by. She didn't see her; she was holding her jaw. And so, the friend got home. She called her up. She said, "What do you mean by ignoring me? I know why you ignored me. You don't like what we're doing!"

The woman said, "What are you talking about?" And the first thing you know, they had a quarrel, and for two years they didn't talk to each other. And the woman didn't even see her. See, one judged another.

You can have the best friend the world, but there're just some things about him that bug you, right? Just bug you to death. And we begin to judge motivation, and that's where you need to be very careful.

You may see a sinner doing some pretty bad things, but you cannot judge why. You cannot think he has all the light he needs, all the grace he needs, everything he needs, and he is making wrong judgment. He may be totally ignorant that this is even wrong, or he may be so blind that he doesn't even see. So, judging, you can't. You can't even judge that anyone went to Hell. Even though they were very, very poor in their spirituality. Because somewhere they may have said, just before they died, in their heart, "Jesus, I'm sorry." You have no way of knowing that.

So do not judge motivation. Do not judge what's in the heart. Because only God could do that. Judge actions. If somebody looks kind of sad, they look sad. You can't put a smile on a sad face no matter how you try. You ever tried to smile when you look sad? You know how you look? Your cheeks go up, and nothing happens. There's no light in your eyes.

We must not judge. And then the Lord won't judge us.

God bless you.

Mixed Mercy

We're going to talk about mixed mercy.

I'm sure you don't know what that means, but mixed mercy to us is that combination in the Scriptures where we know about the justice of God, and then we know about His mercy, and we don't always get the two together.

So we're going to look at the woman at the well (John 4:1–42). You remember her, the Samaritan woman? This is a great, great story because it shows the beauty of God, first of all. He was so tired that day. It says He sat straight down by the well. And the apostles said, "You want to come with us? We're going to go and get some food." And He said, "Nah." He just said, "I'm tired."

I love to see how Our Lord was tired. I guess because I'm tired all the time. I wake up in the morning tired. And when I hear and I see He was so tired, I can relate to that. So He just kind of sat right down, and here comes this Samaritan woman.

Now, the Samaritan woman didn't go to the well that time of day. So, you know she had a few problems. She didn't want to meet the women in their city because they gossiped a lot about her. And so she comes to Our Lord, and she sees Him, and she's a little hesitant. She's over there to get water, and the Lord says to her, "Give me to drink."

And she says, "Oh, here's a real orthodox Jew asking me to give Him a drink." And she thinks, "Something's wrong here." And so she says, "You're a Jew asking me, a Samaritan, a heretic, to give You a drink?"

You know, this is unusual. She's got an idea that she's an outcast. So why is this Man asking an outcast for a drink of water here?

And He says, "Well, if you were to know, you'd ask me, and I'd give you something to drink."

And she looks and says, "You don't even have a bucket."

See how material we are? God speaking way up here, and we're way down here.

And He says, "Ah, whoever drinks the water I'm going to give, you'll never thirst again."

Here she gets very material again. She says, "Ah! I won't have to come to this blessed well and run the risk of running into all these puritanic women. Hey, give me that bucket and give me that water. Great! I won't have to come here anymore."

And then He says to her, "Now, you go and call your husband."

Boy, what a question, huh? And she says, very honestly, "I don't have any."

He says, "Boy, are you right. You've had five." Imagine that. "And the one you live with now isn't even your husband."

And she says, "Oh, I see you're a prophet." Boy, she changed the subject. See, this Man is holy.

I'm going to end the story right there because, you see, we don't understand the love and the mercy of God in our life. We never separate sin from the sinner. If you're a sinner, we just knock you right out of the box until you have a conversion. Then we're going to love you.

But here is Jesus. He's sitting down. He's terribly tired. He sees this woman coming. She's been living with five men. Boom, boom, boom. Knocking them off one at a time. And now the one she's living with isn't her husband, and she's had five husbands—imagine it! And here's Our Lord looking, and He says, "Give me to drink." She had something that He wanted. You see, she's a divorcee, and that's what we're going to address.

I have a lot of experience in that because my mother and father were divorced when I was very young, and I know the terror in the heart of divorcees because they don't understand this Gospel. They don't understand that God calls them to great holiness of life, calls them sometimes to a life of loneliness, because He has a harsh saying here, very harsh in some ways.

In many places in the Gospel, He says, "You can't do that," but when He sees people who have, for whatever reason, He wants to fill that terrible gap, that terrible vacuum, that only those who have been divorced have. There's no way you can sympathize with them, though you can do what you want.

It's like somebody having a leg amputated, and then you give them courage. What do *you* know? You got two legs. You haven't had that experience and that kind of loneliness and that kind of frustration and rejection. See, this woman felt rejected. She was so rejected by the entire city that she just couldn't imagine a holy Man asking her for anything. What did she have to give?

And maybe—do you ever stop to think that maybe the very people in that very village forced her to one marriage after another because of their condemnation, their rash judgment? The poor little woman probably had no way of making a living, keeping her family together. See, you don't know. Sometimes we cause. Sometimes those that are a little weak, they just keep growing weaker and weaker because we were so condemning. We just push them aside as if they were nobodies.

And here we find Jesus with that mixed mercy. He tells it like it is. "Yeah, you're not married, kiddo. You got a problem." See, Jesus always told it like it was. He never, never came out and said, "Oh, come on now, I understand." No, He told it like it was, and because He did, He could afford to temper it with mercy. He could say, "Give me to drink. You have something that I want. You have something I need."

This is a very heartbreaking subject, but we thought we needed to broach it because we want to give you hope. If you're divorced, remember: God loves you. He has a very special love for you. And He holds out His hand to you in great love.

Unity

We're going to talk about unity. First, you're going to see what the Lord says about it.

The Lord says in John 17, "All that I have is yours, and all you have is mine" (v. 10). He's talking to the Father. "And in them," all of you, He's glorified. Then later on, He says, "May they all be one as we are one. May they be one in us. As you are in me, and I am in you." Now, He says, "May they be so completely one"—He's talking about all of you, talking about me—"that the world," here comes the witness, "will realize it is you who sent me" (see 17:21, 23).

Do you realize that the unity you have in your heart, with God and with your neighbor, is a sign that the Father sent Jesus?

And then He says something else. This really gets to you. He says, "And that I love them as much as you love me" (see 17:23).

I want you to realize that this is a mission. The Lord has given every Christian a mission. And what is the mission? The mission is to prove two things: that Jesus is the Son of God and that Jesus loves you in the same way that the Father loves Jesus.

You realize how much love that is? No, you can't realize how much love that is. You'd have to be God. You and I would have to be God to know how much love that is. But isn't it fantastic that the union that God expects of us has to prove two things?

Now, what is union? Well, union doesn't mean we think alike. No way. We're not going to like the same things. I like spinach, and you like carrots. I hate carrots. There's nothing and no one going to make me like carrots. You can fix 'em in a million ways, and to me, they're carrots. They're horrible, orange little things. And nobody is going to make me like carrots. I'll eat them. I don't like them. So there is no unity in carrots or spinach. And we accept that.

There's no unity in ideas because we have different degrees of intelligence.

So, where's unity? Well, there's unity with God. But that doesn't mean I'm going to like what He wants me to do all the time either. You see, realistically, the Lord said there were two sons, and the one went out and did the father's will when he didn't want to, but he did it. So that unity means that I am totally united to God's will. Doesn't mean I like it all the time. Means I do it, I make choices. And sometimes those choices are hard. God asks me to do things I don't want to do, and believe me, He and I have a lot of conversations, some of which I could never tell you about because I don't always like what He asks me to do. But I do it. I grumble a little bit. Sometimes I grumble a lot. But I do it. That's unity.

Now, as I love much and as I grow, I will like what He does. I will say, "Oh, okay, Jesus, I don't care what it is, I'll do it." I can tell you right now I'm not at that point, but I'm going to strive for it.

Unity with you means I accept you as you are because the love of Jesus in me loves you. But I love you as a person. See, I would hate it if you came up to me and said, "Hey, honey, you're horrible, but God lives in you, so I'm going to love Jesus somewhere in you. You get out of the way and let me see the Lord." No, I want you to love me as I am, imperfect, just as I am. And I want to love you the same way, just as you are. When the Father in me loves Jesus in you, that's a spirit. That's love. And it's wherever you are.

Remember, we're all family, and Jesus wants us united so we prove that Jesus is truly the Son of God.

The Commandments

We're going to talk about the law. We're going to look at St. Paul. He says in his Letter to the Romans, "What I mean is that I should not have known what sin is except for the Law. I should not for instance have known what it means to covet if the law had not said 'You shall not covet'" (7:7).

Now, this is true of just about anything. For example, you're going down the street and there's no stop sign there, and you have a feeling that you should stop—it's a four-way street—and so what you're doing is you stop on your own, and you don't mind doing that.

Maybe you've done that for a year, and next time you go, there is a stop sign, and you're angry. "Now I have to stop." See, when you did it on your own, you didn't mind doing it at all. But now somebody said you've got to stop. Now you're all upset.

You know, that's how it is with the commandments. You hear so much about the commandments today that, "Oh, they're so negative."

When I bought the first piece of printing equipment, I got a book—an operation manual, real thick—and it tells you exactly what to do. It tells you what kind of oil to use. It says use this kind of oil, and if you don't, it's not going to work. "So, don't come back to us because we don't have it in warranty if you don't obey this manual." I ain't finding fault with that. I thought, "They know."

I bought a trimmer, and I cannot cut baloney on a trimmer. But I can cut paper on a trimmer. And if I try to cut baloney on that trimmer, it's not going to work.

So, you see, the commandments are the law, and they are just like that. God has made your body; He knows how it operates. He said, "The commandments are your manual." And it says, "These are the things you have to do to keep this machine moving and all the parts in order. Now, if you don't do these things, all of these things are going to happen to you."

See, if I were to write to the Rosback Company and say, "How come I can't cut baloney on a trimmer? I mean, every trimmer should cut baloney!" And they'd say, "Well, it's not made to do that." So when we look at the law, we have to understand that the law is an act of love on the part of God.

The laws of the Church are the same. Now, if I observe them only as a law out of fear—I don't want to go to Hell; I don't want to be frustrated—then we're in trouble. We're in a lot of trouble. We can't keep the law for the law's sake. We can't do that. We must keep the law for love's sake.

And that is where the confusion comes today. They say today sometimes, "Well, if I love, then I don't need to keep the law." No, I keep the law *because* I love. Now, there's a big difference, and the difference is the gift of the Spirit, which is the fear of the Lord, a filial love for God, a childlike love for God, which means, "Lord, if it weren't that I love You so much, I would steal all these cookies."

Now, if I'm going to say I don't want to steal these cookies because I don't want to go down, I guess it's better than nothing, but it's not the real kind of observance that the Church is trying so hard today to get us to perform, to observe the law, to observe the precepts of the Church, to listen to the Holy Father as a child listens to a father.

That's what we must have in our mind. You see, we say, "Holy Mother Church." Every mother has a father. See, you don't have a mother without a father. So when we speak of Holy Mother Church, we're speaking about a relationship that is warm. When we speak about the law, we speak about love.

You obey because you believe that your Father, the One in Heaven and the One the Lord has given us on earth, has the right and the love and the concern to tell us some things to do, those things we don't particularly want to do.

St. Paul had the same problem. He said, "The things I want to do, I don't. The things I don't want to do, ah, those I do" (see Rom. 7:15). So we're all in good company.

Look at the Church as a Mother and remember that the Church enfolds you always in Her arms.

Our Need for God

We're going to talk about our need for God. And no matter who you are or where you are or what you do, you need God.

In Philippians, St. Paul says, "There is nothing I cannot master with the help …" There's where we make our mistakes. Today we have positive thinking, and so all I need to do is think I can do it, and I do it. And St. Paul says, "There is nothing I can do without the help of the One who gives me strength" (4:13). So, without that help, he's saying, "I really can't accomplish a lot."

You know, I've said over and over and over that sometimes our dear Lord asks us to do things that seemingly look a little bit ridiculous. Things that look like, "Well, I can't do this, Lord." Or I'm in a position where it's almost impossible to be virtuous. Or I'm an executive. Or I'm a ditch digger. Or I'm a sports celebrity. And we say, "Well, in this situation, you see, it's so worldly and I'm in the world so much, I really cannot be holy in this situation." And so, what we do is we knock God out of the box.

You could say, "You high school students, well, you just can't be holy." Oh, but you have to be. If you're the only one in school—you know you'd have to ascertain that—but in other words, you don't need to go with the crowd. You don't need to do what everybody is doing because the Lord has given us His Spirit.

And His Spirit is what gives you the strength to do the impossible and the miraculous. And you don't need to always understand the ways of God. He doesn't ask you to understand. If you understood, you'd be God.

You know, faith is a darkness. And because our human nature is always in the process of being more and more human, and you feel so much, you feel from the time you get up in the morning—you don't want to get out of bed, is that right? I don't want to get out of bed. I don't *ever* want to get out of bed in the morning. I can always think of one hundred reasons why I should stay in bed another twenty minutes after that bell almost jolts you out of bed anyway—and so, you're always thinking of ways not to do what the Lord wants you to do, not to be what the Lord wants you to be. But the Lord is giving you a Spirit, and that Spirit is love. And that Spirit enables you to be holy no matter where you are.

A friend of mine is a lawyer, and you don't often think of holy lawyers. I don't know why you never do, but it just seems like politicians—you never think of a holy politician. Have you ever thought of a holy politician? You just don't think of holy politicians. It just doesn't seem to be a place to be holy. But it is! See, we got to change things around. But anyway, this lawyer, whenever I'm in his presence, I do really feel the presence of the Lord. In such a profession, sometimes it's very difficult. But I feel in his presence the Lord Jesus because the Spirit of love and compassion comes through.

And so today, what we want to do is to talk over how to be holy and how to love God and how to be in God and do what you do with God and do it with a kind of freedom and childlike simplicity so that you know that everything you accomplish from the time you get up in the morning, whether you're eating your cereal or going to work or going to school or whatever you're doing, is all, all, all a part of God's part in your life. And we don't want to shut Him out of anything.

Choosing to Be an Image of Jesus

We're going to talk about decisions, how you make them and the capability you have of making the right decision.

You know, today we forget that we're earthenware vessels, or maybe we are very, very aware we're earthenware vessels. We're not very aware, however, of God's power in us. I want to read you just a few little things here.

> And we, with our unveiled faces reflecting like mirrors the brightness of the Lord, all grow brighter and brighter as we are turned into the image that we reflect; this is the work of the Lord who is Spirit. (2 Cor. 3:17–18)

In 2 Corinthians (3:18), St. Paul says that "we with our unveiled faces [reflect] like mirrors the brightness of the Lord." Your face is like a mirror that reflects Jesus. You know what else he says? He says, "You grow brighter and brighter." That image in your face grows every day.

And now this is a very, very important part. He says, "As we are turned into the image we reflect." We call that transformation. We become transformed. That's very important because that is your dignity. And St. Paul says something else here. He says, "Do not model yourselves on the behaviour of the world around you, but let your behaviour change, modelled by your new mind. That's the only way to discover the will of God."

Today we have a lot of old minds running around. An old mind is a mind that just follows the crowd. Why? Because it's the easiest thing to do. See, we overdrink, over-sex, over-everything. Everything is pushed to its ultimate—the reason we have so many diseases today among our youth. You talk about chastity or virginity, people look at you and say, "What are you? You're not with it?" We don't understand what the body is all about. See, *sex* has become a dirty word today, just like *love*. *Love* is almost in some areas a dirty word. You say, "Oh, I love So-and-so. I have such a loving friend."

See, all the beautiful things that God has given us—we have devalued them. Sex has been designed by God to create. What a marvelous thing. If that is your vocation, you participate with the Trinity in bringing forth new life. Just as the Spirit proceeds from the Father and the Son, so children proceed from love. But today, ah! You see, we operate on an instinct level, so we have forgotten the beauty.

Now, I feel like a plumber talking to a bunch of surgeons out there. You say, "Huh? What's that nun talking about sex!" I don't know, somebody told me to get up here and talk about it [*laughs*]. No, but you see, it bothers me because I know the value of your body and soul. And I don't like to see you use it like an animal, that you operate on an instinct level. "I can't help it, I can't help it." Oh, come on, God has given you faculties that are so powerful, they are like

God. So powerful is your will that you can say no even to God.

So, yeah, you can make the right decision. You can stand tall. I think our youth is capable today of standing against the tide. I think our youth today is capable of great suffering and great sacrifice. I think we have a youth that is absolutely tremendous — *if* they know the power of love, the purpose of all the beautiful things God has given us.

It is giving Jesus to each other. And until we understand that, until we do, you may operate on an instinct level that can get pretty bad.

So, don't forget: your body is a temple of the Holy Spirit. Let Jesus just breathe out of you. Let Him radiate so that the image of Jesus grows brighter and brighter in your soul and everyone who sees you sees God. That is your dignity. And you and I don't want to do anything to mar the beauty of His image in our soul.

God bless you, and may your image of Jesus grow brighter.

Loneliness

We're going to talk about loneliness, and I'm going to look at St. Matthew's Gospel, and we're going to see what Our Lord said.

He says, "Foxes have holes and the birds of the air have nests, but the Son of Man has nowhere to lay his head" (8:20). Now, that must have been a terrible thing for the Son of God. After all, He made it all.

Can you imagine seeing yourself building a great big mansion, and you fill it with the most beautiful things that anyone had ever seen? Got that picture? You did the whole thing all by yourself, and somebody takes it over and you're out there about fifty yards away looking at it, and you just don't have a place to go.

You'd say how unjust that is! Well, you see, that's what Our Lord is saying. He created the whole world, and the foxes had holes, the birds had nests, and nobody wanted Him.

Now, loneliness is something everybody has. You can be lonely in a family. You can be lonely in the middle of a thousand people. Because loneliness is something in the heart. And sometimes you're just lonely for God. Sometimes you're just lonely for someone you loved who isn't there. And even though there's fifty other people there, when that one person isn't there, wow, you're just lonely.

Loneliness is part and parcel of our daily life. You may have lost someone, they're dead twenty years now, but every so often, there suddenly comes in your heart a little twinge of loneliness.

I feel that with my mother, who just died recently, and I feel every so often that little twinge of loneliness. She's not in this room, and you go there and you expect her. The other day I went downtown, and I saw a little plant, and I said, "Oh, I think I'll go and buy that for her" and realized there's no one to buy it for. And so you do have that type of loneliness.

Divorcees have a tremendous loneliness because of this terrible, terrible thing that they have to go through. And I know. I went through that with my mother when I was four or five years old. Loneliness is something that we need to relate to God. And we say, "He had it. I have it." And so I take my loneliness, and I say, "Jesus, I'm all with You up there in the mountain all by Yourself."

And you know, there's intellectual loneliness. You get some great idea. Nobody understands. You come out with this big light, this great, great light you've got, and you come out all enthused, and they look at you like, "Eh. What's new?" Or somebody says, "I had that yesterday." Like it's old hat. See?

And then there's a loneliness of people who work in their particular job. Television. You wouldn't think of television producing lonely people. Oh, it does. We had BBC here, and these men come to America, and they spend three months here in this country—three solid months—away from their family, their culture.

We don't think of loneliness. But that's where it is. There's every kind of person today that works in different kinds of jobs that you just wouldn't think about as being terrifically lonely.

And men at sea are lonely. And I hate to say this, but until I met a marvelous priest that's going to be our guest, I never thought of the men at sea. That is awful because there're thousands of them, and we keep forgetting the men at sea. And that means we forget a lot of people. We forget the lonely. We forget all those migrant workers away from their country trying to eke out a living, pulling grapes and tomatoes, and oh, dear Lord.

You know, I think it shows that some of us live in a world that we just have no concern, or we just don't have knowledge, of the tremendous amount of pain and suffering out there, that we just never, never seem to reach.

Remember, Jesus didn't have a place to go. You make a place for your brother and his family.

God bless you.

Stewards

We're going to talk about being a steward.

I have a little passage here from 1 Corinthians. All you people that have Scriptures, look at 1 Corinthians 4. It says, "People must think of us as Christ's servants, stewards entrusted with the mysteries of God" (v. 1).

Now, you and I don't often think of ourselves as being stewards entrusted with the Word of God. I know laypeople don't. How often have you thought you were a missionary? Have you ever thought you're a missionary? Have you ever thought you were entrusted with the Word of God? No, you don't. Most people don't think of themselves as entrusted by God with the Word of God.

Now, the Word of God is manifested not only by what you say but by what you are and what you do. That's very important for us to realize. Because your actions, your compassion, your mercy, your love really say to your neighbor: there is a God and that God must be tremendous. You must, as a Christian, exercise your talents to such a degree that people who don't know God or are real down look at you and say, "What do you got that I don't have?"

Today everything is marketed, isn't it? You go into the grocery store, and the brightest things are what you see first. Well, in the world, we have to market. That's maybe a very poor term to use, but that is all I got. We have to market Jesus.

How? By being like Jesus. By using all your talents. For example, you have three great talents given to you by God. A memory, an intellect, and a will. You say, "That's a talent?" Oh, that's the greatest talent He's given you. You have to manifest to your neighbor that in your memory you don't harbor resentments, anger, and bitterness toward anyone. That shows that you have a tremendous amount of faith. You really believe what you say you are, that you don't let the sun go down on your anger.

You realize God gives you a lot of extra time in the summer? When you have daylight time, you have an extra hour to forgive your neighbor. Did you realize that? Did you never thank Him? I used to thank Him every summer because sometimes it takes me, with my Italian temper, you know, five, six hours extra. I'll look at that sun, and I'll say, "Oh, hold it, hold it. I'm not ready."

And your intellect, you see, there is where we're getting all messed up today. See, we use our reason sometime in the wrong way. Faith sometimes enables us to see things that our reason doesn't. And I've got to give that back to God. See, I've got to say, "Here, Lord, You entrusted me with a talent of reason, and I give it back to You, enhanced by my faith in You."

And then your will. Oh, that's a great thing today. We're all messed up in our wills. Sometimes we decide we're going to play God. Sometime we decide that we're not going to do what He wants us to do and we're going to do our own thing. And our will is very strong; it's just like the spirit—strong. Your will brought you here. Your will said, "I think I'll do this today."

Now, here you are. So you really accomplished something. And that's a talent I have to be able to give to God and say, "Look, Lord, I united my will with Your will." Isn't that tremendous? Isn't that great? I can give it back to God, united, one with His. These are talents, and you and I are stewards. As stewards, we are our brother's keeper. So we're stewards for our brother, you're stewards for your family, you're stewards for yourself, and you're stewards for the world. We must render an account to the Lord when we meet Him as to how we have used the talents that He has given us.

Differences in Spirituality

We're going to talk about being different because you all know you're different. But we don't act like we know that. Especially in our type of spirituality. There are all kinds of spirituality, and we have a tendency today to lump everybody into one specific way of prayer, one specific way of spirituality.

And I want to go over the Gospels with you a little bit more, and you'll find St. Peter, for example. St. Peter was a very impetuous individual, very sanguine, very emotional. And so, what happened was that he acted, and then he thought. And we all know people like that, don't we? And so, the Lord had to work on that poor man three years in order to get him to be some kind of a leader, to be the kind He wanted him to be. He had to really fall hard. He was an emotional man.

Now, here's Paul. He's also emotional, but he's emotional on an intellectual level. He was angry when you didn't understand what he said.

And so here are two men that obviously are different. They prayed different. They acted different.

Now, here's something that we think sometimes: we think here is an economy of spirituality, and you've got to go through all these stages; everybody has to go through all these stages. Well, you see, God isn't held up by anything. He'll say, "I'm going to mess this up. I'm going to do something different." And we find this in the Acts of the Apostles.

Peter didn't want to go to the Gentiles. He was supposed to go to the Gentiles. And he said to the Lord, "Now, wait a minute; don't tell me what to do." The Lord said, "I want you to go." And Peter argues with Him. And when the sheet came down and all the little things in the sheet, he said, "No, I'm not going to eat unclean stuff."

And the Lord said, "Look" — He had to be patient with him, and He said — "don't you call unclean what I just called clean. Now eat it" (see Acts 10:10–15). So Peter was somebody He had to convince over and over and over and over.

So Peter finally goes to Cornelius. I hate to tell you that the first convert was Italian. I just love to admit that. But anyway, here is this man, and he is a convert. He is a Gentile. And so he accepts Jesus.

But you know what happened? Peter says, as he excuses himself to James, after he visited Jaffa and he talked to Cornelius and his whole family, "I had scarcely begun to speak when the Holy Spirit came down on them in the same way it came on us in the beginning [on Pentecost]." He said, "And I remember that the Lord had said, 'John baptised with water, but you will be baptised with the Holy Spirit' " (Acts 11:15–16).

Now, here is a man and his entire family that weren't baptized yet in the Lord, and the Lord came down on Him in the Spirit before He was baptized in water.

And you say, "Well, that's not the way to do it, Lord." But see, the Lord can do what He wants.

And so, sometimes we have that problem. We say, "Well, I like to pray out loud. I like spontaneous prayer." And here's some poor little fella. That's what happens in the family. See, the wife prays spontaneous—oh, she could just take off. I mean, you give her an opportunity, and she'll pray spontaneously for an hour and never stop.

And there's her poor husband, and she says, "Now you pray." And he says, "Well, I don't know what to say." And then she's angry. But see, that man may have an entirely different spirituality. He may speak so deep in the heart that it is beyond words. And that is where we make our mistake. We think the way that we pray is the very, very best way.

Now, it's true—the best way to pray is the way you pray best. But that means just you. Some people love to say the Rosary. They love to say prayers over and over, the same prayer, and they meditate and do all these wonderful things. And some people can't do it at all.

Remember, the way you pray best is the way *you* pray best, and don't worry about anyone else. Because Jesus loves you in a very special way.

Treasure in Heaven

We're going to talk about values, and we're going to see what the Lord has to say first.

He says in St. Matthew's Gospel, "Do not store up treasures for yourselves on earth, where moths and woodworms destroy them and thieves can break in and steal. But store up treasures for yourselves in heaven, where neither moss nor woodworms destroy them and thieves cannot break in and steal. For where your treasure is, there will your heart be also" (6:19–21).

You know, we don't often think of that, but where your treasure is, there your heart is because you think about your treasure all the time. See, you are what your thoughts are. And if your thoughts are not what they should be, then your sense of values is going to go naturally down. We need to look at ourselves and say, "What are my values?"

Well, if your values are just satisfying yourself all day long and all you want to do is what you want to, as it pleases you, you care for no one, then your sense of values is self-oriented. So all you look at is yourself. If your sense of values is others, then you think of others before yourself. And Our Lord is saying to you, "Don't look at the thing that perishes."

You know what I like to look at? Do you ever see these great big trucks pass by, and they have in the back these squashed cars? And there may be a hundred cars on this one trailer, and they're all piled up, one on top of the other. They're rusted, beat up, squashed together. That's a fantastic meditation.

I have an inspiration. And one day, when I get a field camera, I'm going to take the crew out, and I'm going to find one of these pieces of rusty junk that's just all banged up and terrible, and I'm going to stand in front of it, and I'm going to make a one-minute spot, and you know what I'm going to say? I'm going to say, "Does your soul look like this piece of junk?"

Because our values are so poor. When your sense of values gets to the place where all you can think of is the pleasure of this life, that's what a woodworm is going to do. And you have woodworms in your heart because you're never satisfied. You've got one thing; you want two. That's what's wrong. You buy roller skates; now you want a scooter. Then you buy a scooter, and you want a Volkswagen. And then you want to go up, and you're never, never, never, never happy because your heart is not with the Lord. Your heart is not at that place where you can have or not have and be equally happy. So your sense of values is not in the Kingdom; your sense of values is on earth.

In the life of St. Francis, he said he would never own anything. And somebody said, "Well, Father, you got to own your own breviary." A breviary is a prayer book. And he says, "Oh, no. Because if I own my own breviary, then one day I'll have to say to one of the brothers, 'You fetch me my breviary,' and then I'll be afraid of losing it. And then I have to have someone guard it." And then he thought of all the problems that possessions put upon us. Now, he wasn't against having things, but again, we're talking about a sense of values.

Where is your heart? Where is your treasure? Do you get up in the morning just with one thing in mind — "What can I get out of this day? What can I get out of my brother?" — instead of "What can I give today? What can I give my brother? What can I do for you?"

What do you think of when a person comes up to you? You say, "Well, I don't like them. So, if I don't like them, then I'm going to split because why should I talk to anybody I don't like?" Now, your sense of values is all twisted around, see? If our sense of values is with Jesus, then we're going to look at Jesus. We're going to look at Jesus in our neighbor. We're going to look at Jesus in the present situation, and our sense of values suddenly becomes supernatural.

So you've got to get out of the woodworms. You've got to get out of those things that moth consumes. Did you ever have a coat that was wool? You don't use much wool in the South, and yet you go there in the winter time, and you want to put on your coat, and you look at your coat—*ahh!* Full of holes. All gone.

Let's look at Jesus and look at our sense of values. Let's say, "Lord, straighten me out because I want to be with You in Your Kingdom, where You are with me forever and ever."

Our Dignity

We're going to talk about dignity. There're two kinds of dignity that are yours. First is your natural dignity as a son of God but one who is higher than any other animal. I hate to say you're an animal, and we don't want to say that. But I always think that after God created everything, all the animals and all the vegetables and everything else, He had a lot leftover, like a woman that makes a pie.

Did your mother ever do that? Get all those little bits of dough left over? And what does she do? She clumps it all together. This is my idea. Now, Father's going to have apoplexy—he's a theologian—so don't quote me on this, but my idea is that God put all this together, and there you are. And He breathes part of

Himself there, and He says, "Ah, now you can think, you have a memory that's like a computer, a computer as high as the Empire State Building. You can think, you can reason, and then you can will."

That's your human dignity. So, on that level, you're greater than anything else on earth.

Now, you have a supernatural dignity as a Christian, and St. Paul says this, "Examine yourselves to be sure you are in the faith; test yourselves. Do you acknowledge that Jesus Christ is really in you?" (2 Cor. 13:5-6). It's a tremendous, tremendous gift from God that you and I have within us the Spirit of the Lord. To know I have another dignity—and even though you sin, even though we goof off, in spite of the pressures, peer pressure, and the pressures of the world, the rat race you're in.

See, we live in a very affluent society. We live in a society that has everything. Oh, technically we've got it all. We can send a man to the moon—can't cure a common cold—but we can send a man to the moon. We can do all of these great things, and yet I don't think in the history of all mankind has man been so empty inside.

Our Dignity

We've got to ask ourselves why. You've got so much. You can do almost anything you please. And that's the point. You see, we begin to compromise. We yield. We say, "Oh, I can't help this." Oh, yeah, you can. All you need to do is say no. When we forget our dignity, human and supernatural, when we forget all of that, then we begin to yield to the horror of daily life.

I used to have that when I was a kid. When I was a kid, life to me was one big, horrible experience. I hated it. And I used to wonder, "Is this what life is all about? One miserable experience after another? I mean, is there anything more?"

And then I used to think, "God loves me. How come I'm so miserable? How come things get worse day after day after day? Nothing improves. Nothing gets better. Why am I in this rat-race world? Why am I so miserable when I see other kids so happy?" I see them in families, and my parents were divorced. "And why is it that I have it so hard?" And when you get all wrapped up in that horrible, lonely, lonely experience, you begin to lose sight of both dignities. Because if you don't experience the human dignity, you lose that. You just lose it.

Somewhere along the line you say, "Oh, it's a bunch of baloney. And the supernatural dignity, well, if there is such a thing, then how come I'm so miserable?"

So when we lose sight of both dignities, then take it from me: we're going down. And just sometimes that's why we need each other. That's why we've got to be family. We've got to bring the world back so that people can look at us and say, "See how these Christians love one another!" It doesn't mean you only love Christians, but you just love people because they're struggling and heartsick, just like you and me. We all got our problems.

We need to look at ourselves. We need to look at our dignity. The dignity as a human being, our dignity as a child of God, and realize that the Lord said, "Without me, you can do nothing" (see John 15:5). We need to fill our hearts and our souls and our minds with the song of His love, knowing that no matter how difficult life may be, no matter how rotten it gets, God is with us. And because God is with us, we got it made.

That's because God loves you. And don't forget, you are great before Him.

Why People Stay Away from the Church

We're talking about why people stay away from church — inactive members.

I want to read you something from Scripture, and I'm sure you're not going to know how it relates, but I'll explain it to you. Our dear Lord said in St. Matthew's Gospel, and Our Lord had a way of really putting the screws into you — He was very gentle, but oh, sometimes He could let you have it. And so, He says we should not judge so we would not be judged.

But then He says something like this: "Why do you observe the splinter in your brother's eye and never notice the plank in your own?" I'm going to substitute the word *two-by-four* for *plank*. You know what a two-by-four is? Sure you do.

So the Lord is saying, "How come you look at the splinter, a little tiny thing in your finger, in your neighbor's eye, and you don't look at the two-by-four in your own?" That means that you got a lot more than your neighbor has to worry about. He says, "How dare you say to your brother, 'Now, let me take the splinter out of your eye,' when all the time there's a big two-by-four in your own?" (7:3–4).

So what's this got to do with the program? A lot. You know, my mother and father were divorced when I was about four years old. That was one terrible, traumatic experience for me. Awful. I remember when my grandfather said to me, "Rita" — that was my name — he said, "I want you to pray very hard that the judge will let your mother keep you." And I was so scared that I hid behind an icebox. I don't know if you people know what an icebox used to be, now you get refrigerators. But I was behind an icebox, and I hid there because I didn't want anybody to find me just in case I didn't get the right decision. And I stayed there three hours.

And finally, my grandfather came home, and he yelled for me, couldn't find me anywhere. And he said,

"We can keep you!" And I ran on out from behind that icebox. My dear mother and myself had untold agonies from that time on, and I wish I had time to share all the horrors of those years.

One of the horrors of the years was unacceptance. She never married again. That was a terrible penance for her. She really suffered. She was a very loving person and needed someone. But because the Church said no, she never married. You all know, of course, that she became a religious in our order here not too long ago, in '62. God rewarded her. But there were years and years of loneliness. But the worst for me as a child of a single parent was the unacceptance by my neighbor, the unacceptance by kids in my own school.

And I often wondered if I would not have remained in the Church. I never left the Church as such. I loved it and believed in all the things the Church teaches. But I didn't go to church because you just don't want to get hurt anymore. And I wonder if someone would have said to me, "Why don't you come home?"

I wonder if I would have heard anybody, or I wonder if David would have heard—Sister David was her [my mother's] name in religious life—if she would have heard someone say to her, "Look, it's okay. You're all right. God loves you. The Church loves you."

But we never heard that. There was a stigma. And I think that we do not separate sin from the sinner, and we do not give people chances. By golly, if you have done one thing wrong, they're going to put your nose down on the ground, and they're going to twist it. They're almost unhappy if they think God forgives you. You know, you don't mind if God forgives somebody that has hurt you, but you do want God to put the screws on them a little bit, you want Him to break a leg, do something. I mean, you want some proof that God is on *your* side, that He thinks like you do. And He doesn't.

What I'm saying to you is, from my own personal experience, until God Himself really entered into my life, took the initiative—because I wasn't going to take the initiative. In my mind, look, if there was a loving God, by golly, I didn't see Him. I mean, to live in this kind of rat race, horrible kind of existence, with no friends and nobody to care, see? But *you* are the Church. If somebody would have said, "Hey, it's okay. We love you. Come on. We are community." It is that isolationism that the sinner has that, I think, keeps him far, far from the Church.

I think that we are going to always have some kind of excuse not to be an active member of the Church. And we can blame other people. That's the best thing to do, don't you think, to blame other people? That kind of lets you out of your responsibility when you blame other people.

Remember, there is a struggle in life. And you struggle, I struggle. I got a terrible temper—*ahh!*—I'm like that all the time. You and I, all of us together, are struggling. We need you. I need you to say, "Hey, hang in there. We love you." You need us to say the same thing. So hang in there.

And all of you that are struggling, you all come on home.

Living in the Present Moment

We're going to talk about living in the present moment.

There aren't too many people who live in the present moment. You look at yourself and you realize that many, many hours of the day you live in the past or tomorrow. That means that you're mulling over something that you have no control over anymore. Nothing you can do about it. It's like a balloon that you burst. You live in it, you relive it, you say, "I should have done it this way." It's gone, gone, gone, gone, gone. Or you're scared to death of the future. You say, "Oh, this is going to happen, and that's going to happen."

So your whole present moment, like a beautiful new sheet—the Lord keeps giving us a brand-new sheet every moment — and we mar it. You put either old ink or future ink on it, and it's just gone.

And Jesus says a lot of things to us. He says that we should unite. We should get together. We should love each other. And we should agree upon what we love and what we say and what we ask for.

And one of the problems with living in the present moment is we can't even agree amongst each other what we want. If we're living in the present moment, and I'm asking you to pray with me or for me, the Lord is so astounded that if you got two or three people to agree on anything He'd be in their midst.

You know what He says here? He says, "If ... [you] agree to ask anything at all, it will be granted to you by my Father in heaven. For where are two or three meet in my name, I shall be there with them" (Matt. 18:19–20). Sometimes that isn't too hard. But the Lord wants you to know that when you are together, where there is togetherness, there is living in the present moment because you are *in* the present moment. And living in the present moment to me has been one of the greatest helps in my entire life because it kind of takes away the anxiety of yesterday.

St. Paul said one time, "I put aside everything in the past, and I strain forward for what is to come" (see Phil. 3:13). He's straining forward to what is to come. To me, God evolves the present moment.

Some people say, "How do you know God's will?" Well, if it's happening, I got news for you. It's God's will. Whatever is happening—now you may not like it, you may have been the victim of someone else's wrong decision—but there you are. And God wants you to react to that in a most beautiful way. He wants you to react to that in the same way He would and did in His life. And that is what we mean by living in the present moment, watching God like a child. We were asked to be children by the Lord, and God wants us to react to the present moment as a child would, with wonder.

You know, sometimes the Lord seems to pull the rug out from under you. Did He ever do that to you? He does that to me almost every day. You think you're going just great, and you think, "Ah, I got it now! Lord,

I got a handle on Your will! By golly, I know exactly what You want!" The whole thing falls apart. And then you just stand there kind of breathless, and you say, "I thought that's what You wanted." But there's no use. You've got to pick up the pieces. You've got to go on.

You lose someone you love very much. There's nothing to do but to go on. You make a decision on something, and you think it was the wrong decision. But if God permitted it, you know He's going to bring good out of it. There's nothing to do but to go on.

It's that going on when you're not sure. That, we call faith. It takes a lot of faith to live in the present moment. It takes a lot of hope and an awful lot of love.

God bless you.

Children

We're going to talk about children. We're going to talk about children of single parents, single-parent families. We're going to talk about what Jesus thought about children. We're going to find out what we think about them, and their real, real problems.

In St. Mark's Gospel, Jesus says, "Anyone who welcomes one of these little children in my name, welcomes me; and anyone who welcomes me welcomes not me but the one who sent me" (9:37). Sometimes we think, "Well, they're just kids, and they don't know anything. So, you can kind of smack them around a little bit."

He's talking about little children. And today we have so many battered children. So many children who are so mistreated by their parents. We must understand that what you do to a child, you do to Jesus. It's very, very, very strong here.

And then it says, "People were bringing little children to him" (Mark 10:13). That's why I think Jesus must have smiled a lot. You say, "Oh, He never smiled." Oh, come on. No child goes to an old sour face, you know; a child just kind of withdraws. So Jesus had to have not only a pleasant face, but He must have had that smile, that love and compassion that drew children, and parents brought them, and it says, "For Him to touch them." Just touch.

And you know, that's what children need today. They need to be touched, not smacked around. And children of divorced parents have emotional problems. Their sufferings are emotional. They just don't understand. They feel there's something wrong; they feel withdrawn, and they feel rejected, and they just have a lot of problems.

And it says here the disciples, when they saw these kids coming, they just decided to turn them away, yelling, screaming at all the parents bringing all these kids in there. And some of those kids had problems. Just the same as the kids we have today, they had then. And the disciples said, "Ahh! Kids! Get out of here! Go, go, go, go, go!" And Jesus said, "Oh, wait a minute. Let them come. Do not stop them. For it is to such as these the Kingdom belongs" (Mark 10:14). And then it says He put His arms around them.

See how different we are today? Today we have stolen about ten years out of a child's life. He's six, and then he's sixteen. He just hasn't had time to grow up. We just push him and pull him in every direction. She's worried about her hair when she's six years old, screaming and wondering how it looks.

And we have taken away the childlikeness, the adolescence, from children, and some of them have lived very, very long, old lives by the time they're twelve or fourteen. They've experienced almost everything.

And it says here, "[Jesus] put His arms around them and laid His hands on them and gave them His blessing" (Mark 10:16). And you know, some of us have a hard time seeing and believing Jesus would just come and put His arms around some kids. Our concept of Jesus is such a statue, you know, that He was only Lord. But He was also human, and He had that human need to express His love, especially for children. Can you imagine one of those children? I wonder what they grew up to be, those that had God's arms around them? You just wonder.

And we need to look at children today. We need to look and see if you and I have the same kind of special love for children that Jesus had. Do children feel they can come up to us, and do we understand? Are we always yelling and shouting and screaming?

I have to tell you this story. Someone came to me with a big problem, and their kids were yelling and screaming and getting in the way, and then finally the mother swatted one. And a little while later, he came back to me, and he didn't want me thinking ill of his mother. And he said, "Oh, don't pay attention to her. She'll get over it." He loved his mother to a point where he didn't want me to think ill of his mother. Children are very sensitive. They're sensitive to love and a lack of love.

And so, whenever you see a child, whether it's yours or anyone else's, remember what Jesus said: "What you do to the least, what you do to this one, you do to me." Let's keep that in mind and have the same warmth and love and compassion for all children that Jesus had. Remember, they have big problems sometimes.

Mother M. Angelica
(1923–2016)

Mother Mary Angelica of the Annunciation was born
Rita Antoinette Rizzo on April 20, 1923, in Canton,
Ohio. After a difficult childhood, a healing of her
recurring stomach ailment led the young Rita on a
process of discernment that ended in the Poor Clares
of Perpetual Adoration in Cleveland.

Thirteen years later, in 1956, Sr. Angelica prom-
ised the Lord as she awaited spinal surgery that, if
He would permit her to walk again, she would build
Him a monastery in the South. In Irondale, Alabama,
Mother Angelica's vision took form. Her distinctive
approach to teaching the Faith led to parish talks,

then pamphlets and books, then radio and television opportunities.

By 1980 the Sisters had converted a garage at the monastery into a rudimentary television studio. EWTN was born. Mother Angelica has been a constant presence on television in the United States and around the world for more than thirty-five years. Innumerable conversions to the Catholic Faith have been attributed to her unique gift for presenting the gospel: joyful but resolute, calming but bracing.

Mother Angelica spent the last years of her life cloistered in the second monastery she founded: Our Lady of the Angels in Hanceville, Alabama, where she and her Nuns dedicated themselves to prayer and adoration of Our Lord in the Most Blessed Sacrament.